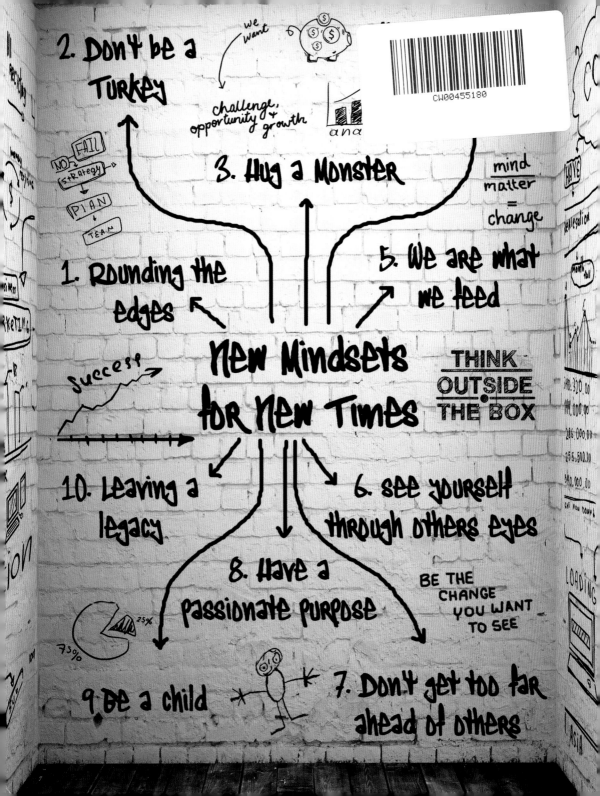

New Mindsets for New Times

2. Don't be a Turkey

we want

challenge, opportunity & growth

3. Hug a Monster

mind / matter = change

1. Rounding the edges

5. We are what we feed

FAIL

NO

Strategy

PLAN

TEAM

Success

THINK OUTSIDE THE BOX

10. Leaving a legacy

6. see yourself through others eyes

8. Have a passionate purpose

BE THE CHANGE YOU WANT TO SEE

25%

75%

9. Be a child

7. Don't get too far ahead of others

LOADING

Typeset in Verdana, CF Jack Story, TrashHand

Published by UK Book Publishing

UK Book Publishing is a trading name of Consilience Media

www.ukbookpublishing.com

ISBN: 978-1-910223-10-9

For Ethan
when his genius has meaning

For Karen
whom I can never thank enough

"Maurice shares his very valuable insight into how mindset sits at the heart of who we are, how we show up and what we can achieve; the mindset we adopt has a strong correlation with success or failure in all that we do. This fabulous book is a straight forward read, and provides many useful take aways that are easy to put into every day practice and can make a real difference. As Maurice says 'if you don't consciously adopt a mindset one will be subconsciously chosen for you'. Choose wisely!"
Alison Hughes, Managing Director, NHS WSYBCSU

"True leadership isn't about seniority, it's about having the right attitude to take the business forward, being recognised and respected by others. Achieving the right mindset is key to successful leadership, and in *New Mindsets for New Times* this critical topic is presented by Maurice Duffy in a refreshing and entertaining format."
Hugo Bagué, Group Executive, Rio Tinto.

"I read this book on the plane home, and it was absolutely brilliant, the perfect airplane read. This is the best book I have ever read on mindset, it distills the wisdom of someone who has worked with the top leaders in business and makes it accessible for everyone."
David Gibson OBE, Visiting Professor, Universities of Derby and Sunderland

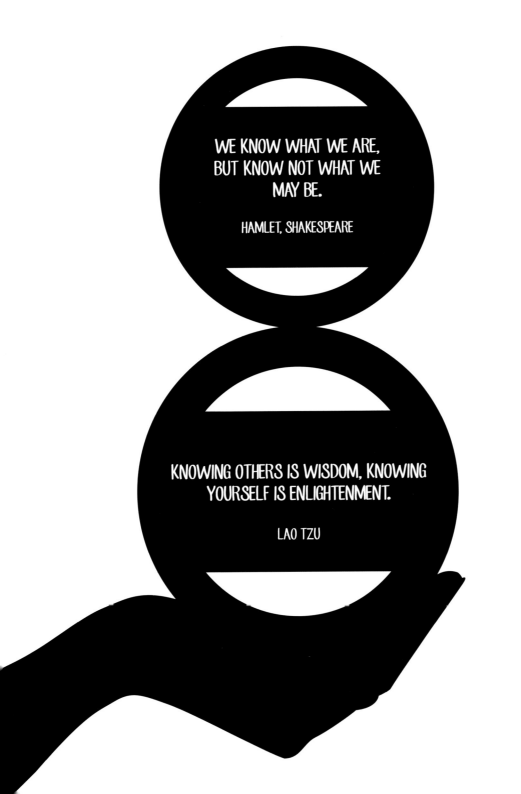

"Go n-éirí an bóthar leat"

THE JOURNEY TO HERE.

As we step forward into the unknown, or at least what is unknown to us, we look for a fair wind and following seas to help us on our way.

There is an old Irish blessing that is quoted by the ancients before any journey begins — Go n-éirí an bóthar leat. This saying is very much part of my Celtic heritage and means 'may the road rise to meet you on the journey you are about to undertake'. I have always interpreted this old saying in my journeys as — the road will rise to meet you if you are prepared to take that first positive step forward.

A core part of my ethos is that things happen when we move forward positively. The world comes to meet us and it will greet us with a smile. This will be a fundamental part of the thinking that I will share with you in what I call this mindset tale.

I have followed an unorthodox career path that has provided me with many opportunities to work in a wide variety of industries. From the world of banking to manufacturing, from corporate land to front line retail, from functional HR to rain-making sales and always at a global level.

I would love to say it was a well-considered pre-planned journey to an ideal final destination. That would be untrue. I will not rewrite history at this stage. I have always tended to do what I enjoy most. I have been lucky to find some great opportunities. Often these opportunities were initially well outside my comfort zone but led me to work on change and business transformation with some remarkable individuals and some great companies.

I do start, however, with learnings from the many failures I have achieved in 30 years of trying to understand human behaviour. I say achieved, as failure helps us achieve. I add to this mix the more insightful learnings gained where I have been fortunate enough to work with, and for, some great CEOs and business leaders who have constantly challenged my decisions, my experiences, my senses, my intuition, and my conclusions.

At Blackswan we have worked with some wonderfully innovative individuals who both teach and practise innovation in the best companies around the world. We have been lucky enough to coach thousands of top leaders and some brilliant CEOs. To the coaches we partner with who share their learnings so willingly, I am adopting your insights and knowledge which have significantly helped to shape my thinking. If I have got it wrong it is totally my fault.

Thirty years of experience, learning and my mistakes have taught me many things. However, I am not for a minute suggesting that these mindsets will deliver a great future. I have no crystal ball and the Irish Catholic in me rebels against that notion.

I will be suggesting over the following pages that if we do not consciously adopt a mindset, one is subconsciously adopted for us, and that we no longer need to be prisoners of our own thinking.

INHIBITIONS ARE DIRECTLY RELATED TO FEAR, AND ARE THE FORCE THAT PREVENT YOU FROM BEING YOU.

CHALLENGE YOUR INHIBITIONS.

WHY IS YOUR MINDSET IMPORTANT?

We see things the way our eyes are instructed to see them. We assume things because of our experiences, our bias and our prejudices. Our mindset controls how we evaluate and react to events around us. What is a mindset? Wikipedia says that a mindset is "a set of assumptions, methods or notions held by one or more people or groups of people which is so established that it creates a powerful incentive within these people or groups to continue to adopt or accept prior behaviours, choices, or tools".

Much of who we are on a day-to-day basis comes from our mindset. Our mindset is the view we have of our qualities and characteristics – where they come from and whether they can change.

Our mindset sets the tone of any engagement with our dreams, aspirations, ambitions, relationships, career, success and happiness. This book is intended to be a wakeup call to change your mindset because:

- Skill and competence are no guarantee of success
- Mindset influences your progress
- You can influence your mindset
- It takes more than guts to succeed
- Strengthen your mindset and strengthen your life

ROUNDING -

Now, to begin with, I have a confession to make to you. At times I am totally inhibited. I fail to act on my dreams for the future. Many times I have to fight my inner demons to stand and present in front of an audience, for example, or to break into a conversation within a group. Yet most people think I am reasonable at doing this. Sometimes I allow myself to become a victim of circumstance when I have the inner capacity and capability to address this challenge.

THE VICTIM MENTALITY CAN RESTRICT AND CONSTRAIN US ALL.

That is my confession to you.

At times, I inhibit myself and my thinking in many ways. It's sometimes called the *spotlight effect*: that exposed, vulnerable, all-eyes-are-on-you inner feeling, that fear to challenge ourselves and commit to action.

'THIS IS YOUR LIFE'

If you've ever clammed up at a meeting (because what if they hate your idea?) or sat out a dance (what if you look like a fool?) or not followed a dream because of fear, or refused to let people see your vulnerability or just kept wishing life would be different and yet you don't know how to fix it, then — this is your life. For those moments when we really are frozen in the spotlight, I have an antidote, a no-fail, one-sentence fix:

Choose the life you want.

YOUR GREATEST TASK IN LIFE ISN'T TO FIND LOVE, BUT TO DISCOVER AND DESTROY ALL THE BARRIERS WITHIN YOURSELF THAT YOU HAVE BUILT AGAINST IT!

Our lives are full of aspirations and desires to 'be' something 'different', something 'better', something 'more'. The challenge for us now at this moment in time is to take the action right here right now to 'be the change we want to see'. This will turn our aspirations and desires into tangible outcomes that allows us to be the person we want to be.

Inhibition is a dangerous barrier if not controlled and overcome. To be inhibited is to be limited, and limited is neither a good way to live or to lead. Now, inhibition is different from prohibition. Prohibition is to be stopped from doing something; it is an outside force. Inhibition is to stop ourselves from doing something. This is a limitation that we impose upon ourselves from within. It prohibits us from being the best we can be.

FEAR TIES YOU DOWN,

DO NOT BE ANCHORED IN THE PAST.

INHIBITION IS TO STOP YOURSELF FROM DOING SOMETHING.

Our fears anchor us to the past. We all worry, fret and stress about whether we are good enough or capable enough to fulfil the expectations of the present, so much so that we often forget we have the ability to shape the future we want.

WE MUST CHALLENGE OURSELVES TO BE MORE THAN WHO WE ARE.

WE MUST
CHALLENGE
OURSELVES TO LIVE
WHAT WE SAY AND
WALK WHAT
WE TALK.

Our most glorious days will be when, out of dejection and despair, we rise to challenge our fears. When we break down our mental barriers, break free of past constraints and breathe new life into ourselves. In this we not only energise and reinvigorate ourselves but also those around us.

CHALLENGE YOUR INHIBITIONS NOW WITH THESE 5 BLACKSWAN 'THINGS TO DO'...

1

ACKNOWLEDGE YOUR FEARS

To eliminate our inhibitions we must understand where they come from. This is done by physically acknowledging them in a notepad, describing them fully, explaining why they are there and how intense they are, forgiving yourself for allowing them to exist and then attacking these mice-sized giants with gusto.

2

DO NOT PARK YOUR INHIBITION

The longer we fail to take action to challenge our inhibitions, the more they grow and become entrenched in our psyche. We must acknowledge them now, expose them in their own spotlight and react positively to them. We will gain strength from this challenge and will be better equipped to tackle similar challenges we may face in the future. We can experience elation from conquering our inhibitions. Try it. Today.

③

TALK ABOUT THEM

Sharing our fears and concerns is very therapeutic and builds confidence. Positive friends and advisors can be incredibly supportive. We must surround ourselves with people who we can learn from, challenge us and give us energy.

ATTACK THE FEELING

Figure out what is holding you back and address those specific concerns. Over-exaggerate positive responses to your actions to build your confidence. Be fearless, not fearful, in the actions you take.

5

FAKE IT UNTIL YOU MAKE IT

We are all performers. You must move to the person you want to be. Go there. Stay there. **PRACTISE, PRACTISE, PRACTISE** until you become the change you want to see. Of course, it may feel uncomfortable, but I would prefer to be uncomfortable and learning, than be a captive within a box of my own making. Don't let others around you, with preconceived ideas of who you are, inhibit this effort.

WORRY IMMOBILISES YOU; WORRY GIVES SMALL THINGS A BIG SHADOW.

MINDSET
TWO

DON'T BE

A TURKEY

WE CANNOT EXTEND THE PAST INTO THE FUTURE AND WE CANNOT CHANGE OURSELVES IF OUR THINKING IS ANCHORED IN THE PAST.

Sitting in the relative calm of the West Coast of Ireland I first happened upon Lewis Carroll's *Through the Looking Glass*, and was struck by when the White Queen tells Alice that in her land, "memory works both ways". Not only can the Queen remember things from the past, but she also remembers "things that happened the week after next". Alice attempts to argue with the Queen, stating "I'm sure mine only works one way... I can't remember things before they happen". The Queen replies, "It's a poor sort of memory that only works backwards".

How much better would our lives be if we could live in the White Queen's kingdom, where our memory would work backwards and forwards? F. Scott Fitzgerald once said...

THE TEST OF A FIRST-RATE INTELLIGENCE IS THE ABILITY TO HOLD TWO OPPOSED IDEAS IN MIND AT THE SAME TIME.

In Nicholas Taleb's book *The Black Swan* he tells the story of a turkey's life. From being born into comfort, being cared for and fed every day by the farmer, the turkey's life is a good one. That turkey sits there and thinks *'when I analyse my life every piece of data that I extrapolate based upon current and historic trends tells me that I have a great life'.*

However, what the turkey neither knows nor can the data tell him, that tomorrow is December 24th and that turkey will become someone else's lunch.

As a West Coast of Ireland boy, all the symbols, artefacts and rituals are of a history past. In my generation we were constantly reminded of our heritage, our history and to an extent the English domination of our small island. Of course history and experiences are important but we cannot allow the past to dominate the present or control the future. The past can teach us for the future, but I kindly suggest that it can only give you some general indicators and should be but one piece of a future-orientated puzzle. We should not allow the past to determine the future.

I remember sitting listening to Father Brian D'Arcy a priest I admire, on our national TV station RTE, when he said **"there is a reason why your car has a big windshield and a small rear-view mirror. You are supposed to keep your eyes on where you are going, and just occasionally check out where you have been"**. The past to me is a place of reference not a place of residency.

we tend to accept that our current circumstances are heavily influenced by our genetics, culture, and past decisions. So here is a challenging question: "When does the future determine the present?" You too must challenge yourself and your assumptions.

NOTHING THAT YOU ASSUME TO BE TRUE AND NOTHING THAT YOU HAVE EXPERIENCED TO DATE MAY BE TRUE IN THE FUTURE.

5 THINGS TO DO

SO YOU'RE NOT THE TURKEY!

ASSUMPTIONS ARE NOT REALITY

Assumptions are always the starting point but we should always remember they are static points in time and need to be revisited, tested, questioned, discarded, modified and validated. There are two sets of assumptions: those that we consciously make and those that we subconsciously make. We need to always question, assess and stress test what we think, as although our assumptions may represent our reality, we must always remember that they sometimes lack factual basis and can totally mislead us.

BIASES CAN MISLEAD YOU

As thinking, feeling human beings, we are a cocktail of emotions and feelings that can sometimes cloud our thinking and produce bias reactions which we often confuse with facts. Bias is usually based more on feelings and opinions rather than on facts. Our experiences throughout our life will affect our outlook on similar situations. Just as Pavlov's dogs reacted to the sound of a ringing bell and automatically associated it with food, people associate familiar sights, sounds, smells, actions and thoughts with how they should act or think as well as what is to follow. Sometimes it only takes a single event to occur for a person to develop a strong opinion and develop a false sense of what is reality. We have to remember that the past is not the future. Always ask yourself "what is the reality?"

SOMEONE'S DEFINITION OF YOU DOESN'T DEFINE YOU

In 1979, as a sophomore in high school, a young basketball player was cut from the varsity team. He was devastated but he wasn't done. Three years later in 1982 he made the game-winning shot in the NCAA championship game. In 1984 he was passed over by the first two teams in the NBA draft but he went on to become arguably the greatest basketball player of all time. Michael Jordan epitomises the fact that another person's opinion doesn't have to be your reality. Oprah, Muhammad Ali, Walt Disney, J.K.Rowling, Gandhi and countless others have been mislabelled, misunderstood, and overlooked at one point or another in their lives. **Be yourself - everyone else is taken.** Be the person you want to be, a person who lives their aspirations rather than dreams of them.

BUILD CAPACITY AS WELL AS CAPABILITY

I am always surprised by the drive from people to build increased capability without understanding that you must also build capacity. One of my favourite lines in workshops is that you must unlearn before you learn. We must build both a capacity for the future as well as a capability. We cannot keep trying to cram stuff in until we release ourselves from what is holding us back.

LEAD YOUR BRAIN TO THE FUTURE

We are conditioned to see the world in a certain way. Once we understand the importance of our past conditioning we experience a paradigm shift in the way we see things. To make large changes to our lives we must work on the basic paradigms through which we see the world.

The bottom line is that you must *want* to change in order for any change to take place. You must be at a place in your lives where you are motivated to take the necessary steps towards making a needed change. Then you must tell your brain that you are going to change and you are not going to allow the experiences of the past or your inhibitions to get in your way.

WHEN PEOPLE UNDERMINE YOUR DREAMS, PREDICT YOUR DOOM, OR CRITICISE YOU, REMEMBER, THEY'RE TELLING YOU THEIR STORY, NOT YOURS.

HUG MONSTER

IT'S NOT THE MISTAKES AND FAILURES YOU HAVE TO WORRY ABOUT, IT'S THE OPPORTUNITIES YOU MISS WHEN YOU DON'T EVEN TRY THAT HURT YOU THE MOST.

Many times as I stalked the corporate corridors, or paths of my life, decisions were presented to me and I'm embarrassed to say that I took the easy road. Many of us want an easy life and are neither thrill seekers nor fear junkies. Yet even in the comfort of being ordinary we are often presented with a route to our dreams.

I'VE CERTAINLY MADE MY SHARE OF EXCUSES WHEN IT COMES TO STEPPING OUT OF DIFFICULT DECISIONS WHEN I SHOULD HAVE STEPPED IN, BUT EACH TIME I'VE CHOSEN TO STEP IN TO CONFRONT MY DEMONS I HAVE BEEN ENRICHED.

I remember when I first met Rebecca Stephens back in 1996 after she had completed her ascent as the first British woman to climb Everest. I was so impressed and in awe of someone that brave, that daring and that adventurous. She had a 'fear not' approach to following her dream.

I also recall hearing that there are 365 'fear-nots' in the bible, one for every day of the year. It was even mentioned in the movie *Facing the Giants*. Now I have not studied the bible to that extent but what strikes me every time I meet extraordinary ordinary people who continue to do great things, is that the courage, the 'fear not' attitude that some people have, drives them to overcome great challenges and to face down their demons. Because you know what, we all have demons buried sometimes very deep within ourselves.

I WONDER AND WORRY ABOUT WHAT WE KEEP HIDDEN FROM THE WORLD. FIGHTING DEMONS DOES NOT JUST MEAN RIGHTING WRONGS AND EXPOSING YOUR SKELETONS. IT ALSO ENTAILS FIGHTING THOSE MONSTERS UNDER YOUR EMOTIONAL BED THAT KEEP YOU FROM BEING ABLE TO LIVE YOUR DREAMS.

TO GET SOMETHING
YOU'VE NEVER
HAD, YOU MUST DO
SOMETHING YOU'VE
NEVER DONE.

I recently re-read Alex Pattakos' book *Prisoners of Our Thoughts*. He captures comments from the wonderful Viktor Frankl as he describes his time in the death camps of Nazi Germany where he watched men walk through the huts comforting others, giving away their last piece of bread. "They may have been few in numbers" he wrote, "but they offer sufficient proof that everything can be taken from man but one thing: the last of human freedoms—to choose one's attitude in any given set of circumstances, to choose one's own way".

WE ALL DO HAVE A CHOICE.

We can choose an inner dialogue that drives self-encouragement, self-motivation and a 'can do' attitude to life. Yet many of us choose one of self-defeat, self-pity or acceptance that where we are is OK. The battle for our brains is between what our subconscious decides for us or what we decide for ourselves. We have the power to choose. The key is to realise that it's not what happens to us that matters; it's how we choose to respond.

THE LOUDEST AND MOST INFLUENTIAL VOICE WE HEAR IS OUR OWN INNER VOICE, OUR SELF CRITIC HOLDING US BACK.

This inner voice can work for us or against us. It can enable us or hinder us. It can allow us to be optimistic or pessimistic. It can wear us down or it can cheer us on. We get to decide. We can consciously adopt a mindset or one will be subconsciously adopted for us.

"This is the true joy in life, the being used for a purpose recognized by yourself as a mighty one; the being thoroughly worn out before you are thrown on the scrap heap; the being a force of Nature instead of a feverish selfish little clod of ailments and grievances complaining that the world will not devote itself to making you happy."

GEORGE BERNARD SHAW

5 THINGS TO DO WHEN HUGGING A MONSTER

ATTITUDE CAN SET YOU FREE

Let's adopt a "f&%#-it!" attitude. I apologise for the language but I do want to make a serious point. This attitude doesn't mean total surrender or not caring about yourself and others. It doesn't mean not trying your best or giving up. It definitely doesn't mean bailing out on life and moving to a deserted island. In my world it means the absolute opposite; it enables you to engage more deeply in your life. It liberates you to do so because it allows you the freedom to do what you want, and what you want is a better version of you.

LET THE WORLD COME TO MEET YOU

I often use the expression: what makes people poor?

They **P**ass **O**ver **O**pportunity **R**egularly. Luck doesn't just happen. Not most of the time, anyway. Luck happens to people who go looking for it, and who are ready for it when it comes. People talk about being in the right place at the right time. And that is the thing about luck: in order to be in that place at that time, sometimes you have to stand in lots of different places (or the same place lots of different times).

When it comes to creating your own luck,
Richard Wiseman said:

MY RESEARCH REVEALED THAT LUCKY PEOPLE GENERATE GOOD FORTUNE VIA FOUR BASIC PRINCIPLES. THEY ARE SKILLED AT CREATING AND NOTICING CHANCE OPPORTUNITIES, MAKE LUCKY DECISIONS BY LISTENING TO THEIR INTUITION, CREATE SELF-FULFILLING PROPHESIES VIA POSITIVE EXPECTATIONS, AND ADOPT A RESILIENT ATTITUDE THAT TRANSFORMS BAD LUCK INTO GOOD.

So a key part of serendipity is knowing what direction you want to go in, and being open to new opportunities as you move along that path. This means that you are focused on your goal, but are mentally open and ready to embrace new ideas. Put it this way; if you were on a premiership football playing field, it would render you ready to receive the ball and execute a great move, rather than make a sideways, ineffectual pass.

ELIMINATE MENTAL PARADIGMS

Life does not just happen to us. Yes we are creatures of habit. We do rely heavily on learned thinking patterns. As these thinking patterns become more and more automatic we start thinking more and more that this is the way things are. We lock ourselves inside our own mental prisons. Physician Deepak Chopra captured it when he said, "We erect and build a prison and the tragedy is that we cannot even see the walls of this prison". These mental paradigms and the models of unreality which underpin them deny us the opportunity to change 'life happening to us' to 'we happen to life'.

'VEDANTA TREATISE'
APPLY AN ART, A SKILL AND A TECHNIQUE

The book by A. Parthasarathy, *Vedanta Treatise: The Eternities*, looks at ancient philosophies no longer taught today, which consider the knowledge of self. There are three main disciplines which constitute this technique, they are: Concentration, Consistency and Cooperation. The discipline of concentration is keeping your mind focused on the present action. The discipline of consistency is maintaining your direction towards your goal and the third discipline is to recognise and maintain the spirit of cooperative endeavour. The ancients knew a thing or two about well-being in the mind and soul.

BE FEARLESS, NOT FEARFUL

If you can keep your head when all about you
Are losing theirs and blaming it on you,
If you can trust yourself when all men doubt you,
But make allowance for their doubting too;
If you can wait and not be tired by waiting,
Or being lied about, don't deal in lies,
Or being hated, don't give way to hating,
And yet don't look too good, nor talk too wise:

If you can dream—and not make dreams your master;
If you can think—and not make thoughts your aim;
If you can meet with Triumph and Disaster
And treat those two impostors just the same;
If you can bear to hear the truth you've spoken
Twisted by knaves to make a trap for fools,
Or watch the things you gave your life to, broken,
And stoop and build 'em up with worn-out tools:

If you can make one heap of all your winnings
And risk it on one turn of pitch-and-toss,
And lose, and start again at your beginnings
And never breathe a word about your loss;
If you can force your heart and nerve and sinew
To serve your turn long after they are gone,
And so hold on when there is nothing in you
Except the will which says to them: "Hold on!"

If you can talk with crowds and keep your virtue,
Or walk with Kings—nor lose the common touch,
If neither foes nor loving friends can hurt you,
If all men count with you, but none too much;
If you can fill the unforgiving minute
With sixty seconds' worth of distance run,
Yours is the Earth and everything that's in it,
And—which is more—you'll be a man, my son!

Rudyard Kipling

HE WHO CANNOT REASON IS A
FOOL; HE WHO WILL NOT IS A BIGOT;
HE WHO DARES NOT IS A SLAVE.

WILLIAM DRUMMOND

NURTURE YOUR MIND WITH GREAT THOUGHTS; TO BELIEVE IN THE HEROIC MAKES HEROES.

BENJAMIN DISRAELI

DON'T

BOTTLE IT...

I DESTROY MY ENEMIES WHEN I MAKE THEM MY FRIENDS.

ABRAHAM LINCOLN

We all know that feeling when we meet someone and we just know we are going to like them. Our impression process kicks in naturally, in every new situation. Within the first few seconds people subconsciously pass judgment on us — and we subconsciously pass judgment on them — both of you looking for common surface clues. Once the first impression is made, it can be difficult to change.

I remember when Joe meets with Alice for the first time. In their initial conversation Joe found Alice to be particularly quick witted with great energy in her thinking and speaking. As this is a surface characteristic Joe greatly admires, Joe subconsciously credits Alice with several other characteristics, such as being bright, intelligent, creative and articulate. Joe has no rational basis for these assumptions and Alice may never have these qualities. It is simply that Joe wants to like her and associates quick wittedness with these qualities. I call this a halo bias, also known as the physical attractiveness stereotype or the "what is beautiful is good" principle. The halo effect, at the most specific level, refers to the habitual tendency of people to rate attractive individuals more favourably for their personality traits or characteristics than those who are less physically attractive. Our bias can be extremely, and unreasonably or illogically, powerful.

The opposite of the halo effect can also arise. One bad quality or experience can cloud your view of a person's better qualities. This is known as the 'devil' or 'horn' effect. We often make impressions from a distance, without ever speaking to someone and, of course, we should not 'judge a book from its cover'. Many times in our lives then, we are limiting our experience with others or limiting their experience with us. We must remember that we create the reality of our interactions with others according to the perception we have about them. We must all refresh our perceptions constantly.

EVERYTHING THAT IRRITATES US
ABOUT OTHERS CAN LEAD US TO AN
UNDERSTANDING OF OURSELVES.

CARL JUNG

Of course, others are also being driven by their biases which impact their perception of us. There are many things we can do that will bin some of their biases. Marcia Grad in her book *Charisma: How to Get That Special Magic* summarises them in SOFTEN — that allows you to show your interest and bin their biases.

S Smile at the world and the world will always smile back at you.

O Open your body language and allow others to see that you are opening yourself up to them.

F Forward lean so that people can see your interest.

T Touch in a non intrusive manner and it will create a good impression and physical connection.

E Eye contact that is open and wide almost allows people to see into your soul.

N Nod at appropriate times and it indicates listening and interest.

You can even change your experience with others simply by changing the way you perceive them. If you bottle up your perceptions you can close out others who may be hugely helpful to us. If we allow our prejudices, perceptions and biases to control our thoughts, we are shutting out opportunities to embrace great and new things. Don't bottle up these feelings. Bin them now.

5 WAYS TO BIN IT!

GIVE AWAY THAT WHICH
YOU WANT MOST

As we live our lives we want people to trust us, to like us, to engage with us, to be authentic with us, to be our friends, to be our confidants, to not judge us harshly, to listen to us, to laugh with us, to not speak ill of us and to generally be nice to us. So we need to give to others **TRUST, AUTHENTICITY, FRIENDSHIP** and **RESPECT.**

TREAT ALL PEOPLE LIKE V.I.P

People are valuable and important, yet we forget to understand that value because we do not listen with humility, our ego is constantly looking for self-gratification and we forget to acknowledge the small things in life such as thank you, please, and sincere appreciation. I always tell leaders to lead without a title and to make a conscious effort to remember these things.

BE THE FIRST TO GIVE

In order to influence and engage people we must be the first to give without looking for any reward. Those who are looking for immediate response always wait a long time. We must be first to give our trust, our engagement and our friendship.

LISTEN LIKE A GENIUS

We all know that feeling. We are speaking to someone and we just know they are not listening. Do you think people have that experience with you? Your mind drifts or someone more interesting appears and you are gone in mind, even if your body has not moved. You must give total attention to the person you are speaking with.

FOCUS ON VALUE GENERATION NOT EGO GRATIFICATION

Too often value to us is what we do and not what the other person gets. We are sometimes so busy bumping into our own ego that we cannot see the wood for the trees. We tend to focus on what we do, all those activities that are so important to US and that have no benefit whatsoever to the other person, be it a customer or a friend. We need to understand that we are not born just once on the day our mothers give birth to us, but...life obliges us to examine our inner SELF and review, renew and recalibrate who we are, as we grow, mature and learn.

COMMON SENSE IS THE COLLECTION OF PREJUDICES ACQUIRED BY AGE EIGHTEEN.

ALBERT EINSTEIN

A MAN IS BUT THE PRODUCT OF HIS THOUGHTS – WHAT HE THINKS, HE BECOMES.

MAHATMA GANDHI

WE ARE

I had the pleasure of working for Nortel Networks when it was great. I remember running a major conference in Miami and watching a traditional native Indian dance.

Later one of the dancers told me this story. I have heard it many times since, but it still is a powerful truth for us all...

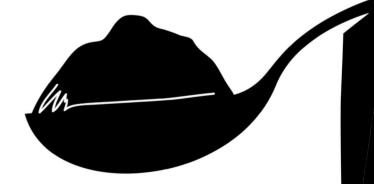

An old Cherokee chief is teaching his grandson about life.

"A fight is going on inside me," he says to the boy. "It is a terrible fight and it is between two wolves.

"One is evil - he is anger, envy, sorrow, regret, greed, arrogance, self-pity, guilt, resentment, inferiority, lies, false pride, superiority, self-doubt, and ego.

"The other is good - he is joy, peace, love, hope, serenity, humility, kindness, benevolence, empathy, generosity, truth, compassion and faith.

"This same fight is going on inside you - and inside every other person, too."

The grandson thought about it for a minute and then asked his grandfather, "Which wolf will win?"

The old chief simply replied, "The one you feed."

(unknown)

MY QUESTION HERE IS SIMPLE.

Do we ever consider what we are nurturing within ourselves? I would not regard myself an overly spiritual person but there are many things I believe we can learn from the ancients. Buddha recommends that we cultivate the opposite of our weakness, and I advocate this approach in many programmes I run.

FOCUS ON YOUR STRENGTHS.

Stretch them as far as you can and they will help minimise or eradicate our weaknesses. St. Paul said, "whatever is true, whatever is noble, whatever is right, whatever is pure, whatever is lovely, whatever is admirable — if anything is excellent or praiseworthy —think about such things". Yet we waste so much time, energy and angst on negative energy. We are what our minds eat. What are you feeding yours?

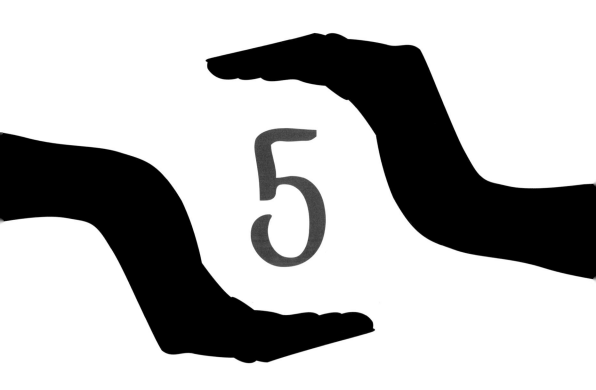

5
THINGS TO DO
TO NURTURE
YOURSELF TODAY

FOCUS ON WHAT YOU THINK

It is important that you surround yourself with positive people and positive things. Too often we allow ourselves to be so consumed by other people's negativity that it contaminates our thinking and restrains us within bars of our own making. We must, must...

"Watch your thoughts, for they become words.
Watch your words, for they become actions.
Watch your actions, for they become habits.
Watch your habits, for they become character.
Watch your character, for it becomes your destiny"

Unknown Author

2

FILTER OUT THE NEGATIVE

The truth is that we are not our thoughts. I work with a charity that I care a lot about, PSPA, as my mother-in-law suffers from an aggressive strain of this condition. I remember in one of the seminars being surprised to discover that our brains produce 70,000 thoughts every single day! Blimey! So our brains are constantly filtering our thoughts. We do have a choice about what we think. Either we listen to the thought and allow it to trigger a whole host of other negative thoughts, or we challenge the thought and drive it from our thinking.

3

CHANGE YOUR MIND MOOD

I find that sometimes I feel down, tired, lethargic and my brain tells me that I need food, drink or some stimulus to give myself a lift. For someone like me who struggles with weight that is the worst possible solution. Instead, we can tell our brains to be happy. We can lift our own spirits. Yet too often it is comforting to feel blue. For me to run, to play with my young son, are the exhilarating moments. Find your positive space and go there. Do not allow your brain to tell you how you are feeling.

RELAX YOUR MIND

I struggle with shutting my brain down. I admire tremendously those who can be still, listen attentively to music, or just watch a beautiful space. We have to make a commitment to our brain to give it time to relax. We have to bring that mental focus to relaxation and teach ourselves to control it, otherwise it will control us. For me this is tough.

SHOW YOUR INNER SELF

I ran a workshop at the Wirral in North West England on personal change, and one of the things I asked the participants to do was build a physical representation of the journey they had been on. They selected a mirror for themselves. Later that night I drafted these words to go with that Wirral mirror and to say - do we really question who we are?

Look In The Mirror.
When you struggle for your self,
And you wonder what to do,
Look at your reflected self
And see what it says about you

Go to the mirror
And take a really hard look
At what that reflection
Tells you about you

It is not your parents, partner or friends
Whose judgment you must pass,
The person who holds you in the past
Is the one staring right back from the glass

The person whose verdict
counts most in your life
Is the one you keep hidden
And well out of sight

The person in the mirror
is the real picture of you
And you have passed
the most difficult test
when that person is the one
you show to the rest
as the mirror never lies
if we are failing the human test

Mirror mirror on the wall
Are we being true at all
Mirror Mirror on the wall
Are we taking the opportunity to change
One bit at all

Mirror mirror on the wall
Now is my chance
To show them all

Humility, humanity
Trust and great belief
And that no dream is too extreme
To be the best I can be.

Cannot claim total credit as this is a mixture of recall and original work.

See

YOURSELF THROUGH OTHERS EYES

SOMETIMES YOU CAN'T SEE YOURSELF CLEARLY UNTIL YOU SEE YOURSELF THROUGH THE EYES OF OTHERS.

ELLEN DEGENERES

I was recently asked to meet with an exceptionally bright young Executive, who had achieved a 1st everywhere he went and was on a fast track career plan. I was asked to meet this young man to establish if he needed coaching. Now, I honestly think that in 25 years of being involved with Leadership development I had not met a more egotistical, self-absorbed individual, with such a deep lack of self-awareness or respect for diversity. The challenge for me was holding a mirror to this person and being prepared to give him real world feedback. The challenge for him was being receptive to what I said.

No person is an island and we should always hold a mirror both to ourselves and to our impact on others. The challenge many of us face is that we react to criticism, judgment or rejection as if it were a threat to our survival. Yet if we allow ourselves to, we can learn a lot about ourselves from the people we surround ourselves with and the relationships we have. Real friends, if used wisely, are invaluable for the support and encouragement they offer. They have a unique ability to give us a new perspective on ourselves. I remember sitting for the first time with my wife Karen in a restaurant in Spain and sharing my life's story. I remember it so well — as it was probably the first time I did not airbrush passages of history through rose-tinted glasses. For that dialogue to happen, I had to be willing to put aside my ego, trust our relationship and ask for sincere input. Sincere reflection requires humility. Our relationships with others give us the unique privilege of seeing ourselves through someone else's eyes.

I have learned a lot from Paulo Coelho's work and have read many of his books. I can re-read them many times and still continue to learn from them. Here is an excerpt from *The Alchemist*:

The Alchemist picked up a book that someone in the caravan had brought. Leafing through the pages, he found a story about Narcissus. The Alchemist knew the legend of Narcissus, a youth who daily knelt beside a lake to contemplate his own beauty. He was so fascinated by himself that one morning he fell into the lake and drowned. At the spot where he fell, a flower was born, which was called the narcissus.

Looking in the mirror and seeing yourself through your own eyes does not give you objective feedback. Even as adults, our nervous system still equates emotional safety with physical safety, even if conceptually we understand the difference. In particular, if we have experienced significant trauma (which unfortunately is true for so many) or emotional challenges that are similar to an event we are now facing, interpretations of threat are soft-wired into our nervous system so we experience sensations of not being safe that arise before any thought is conscious.

However, I always start from the premise that whatever we do, we do for a good reason. Even if it is cloaked in bad behaviour, we do what we do because—at some level—it does something good for us. Perhaps it makes us feel better. Perhaps it moves us forward. Perhaps it holds someone else back (thus potentially moving us forward by default). No matter the situation, no matter the scale, scope or location, each of us will do what (we think) serves us best. The trick is figuring out if we are doing this because of lack of thought, our inner demons, our inhibitions, or our sheer self-interest and understanding and accepting its impact on others.

IF WE FIGURE OUT SELF-INTEREST, WE FIGURE OUT EVERYTHING.

WAYS OF SEEING YOURSELF THROUGH THE EYES OF OTHERS

UNDERSTAND THAT OTHER PEOPLE ARE YOUR MIRROR

Too often when we look at the world, we forget that we are surrounded by fantastically wonderful brains which are deciphering our messages, reading our body language, interpreting our words, analysing our intents, judging our integrity, shaping opinions of us, profiling our personalities, and self-checking our and their realities. A huge, complex, and diverse series of brains surround us and they are a much better source of deciphering who we are than we are. Use them and we will get the input we need to flush out our demons, challenge our versions of realities and become much more rounded individuals.

PEOPLE SAY THINGS FOR A REASON

Recognise that people say things to you, or about you, for a reason. We must be open to input and feedback. I think we can all agree on that. If we are receptive to comments and responses from others, then conflict resolution and trust building happens almost by magic. However, being too prone to responding defensively to feedback is a problem for many of us. For me, it is a major challenge when I think that what someone is saying does not align to what I see as 'my truth'. My truth being my version of events. This drives my desire to prove my innocence. I am well aware that this can be detrimental to healing, engagement and reconciliation yet my immediate, hard-wired response is to defend myself. When we act in defence, we are neither open to ourselves nor to the other person. Instead we are consumed with the intensity of wanting to be seen as the well-meaning people that we believe ourselves to be. We have to give others space and check our responses for intent, integrity and balance.

DON'T POINT FINGERS

Remember, when you point your finger accusingly at someone else, you have three fingers pointing at yourself.

No one is so blind as the man who refuses to see. When you blame others, you give up your power to change. It is much easier to see the failings of others than to see our own. Whilst running change programmes, I often see that people are very quick to tell me how others need to change, but very slow to identify and address their own immediate needs to change. Change must start with you. As the old saying goes 'people in glass houses should not throw stones'.

BE MORE BEAUTIFUL
THAN YOU THINK

On April 15, 2013 Dove launched a video entitled "Dove Real Beauty Sketches". The video went viral and was widely talked about. In the video, a small group of women are asked to describe their faces to a person whom they cannot see. The person is a forensic artist who is there to draw pictures of the women based on their verbal descriptions. A curtain separates the artist and the women and they never see each other. Before all this, each woman is asked to socialise with a stranger, who later separately describes the woman to the forensic artist. In the end, the women are shown the two drawings, one based on their own description, the other based on the stranger's description. Much to their amazement and delight, the women realise that the drawings based on strangers' descriptions depict much more beautiful women. The video ends: "You are more beautiful than you think".

BE THE PERSON YOUR DOG THINKS YOU ARE

I saw this phrase on a car bumper sticker and it made me think about how dogs interact with people. I have two dogs that love me. They behave towards me as if I was the greatest thing in their lives. Each morning without fail they embrace me with a joy and welcome that is motivating and uplifting. They never question my motives. They give unquestioning loyalty. They give me their total trust. Their greatest joy is in playing with me. They will always protect me at all cost. They ask for little in return and are always waiting for my return. Be the great person your dog thinks you are.

MINDSET SEVEN

DON'T GET TOO FAR AHEAD OF OTHERS

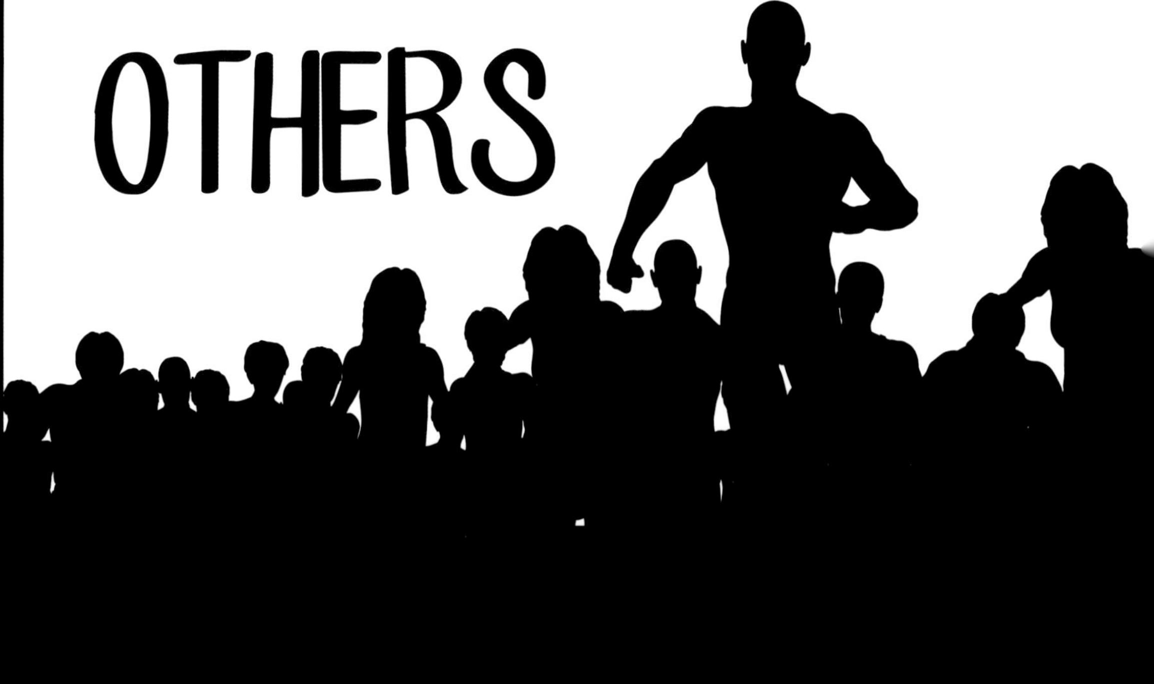

I am often asked to talk about future trends and sometimes get accused of not understanding people's current reality. The challenge of change is to articulate a future that people can see — one that is not so distant that they cannot imagine it ever being there.

If we cannot fire people's **imagination** with where we are going, yet hold their **attention** to explain the journey, and engage the senses that this could be their reality, they will not listen or engage with us.

Tom Davenport and John Becks conducted an experiment which was reported in the Harvard Business Review where sixty executives were assessed on what provoked their interest. Overall the factors most highly associated with getting attention in rank order were: the message was personalised; it evoked an emotional response; it came from a trustworthy source, or respected sender; and it was concise. The messages that both evoked emotion and were personalised were more than twice as likely to be attended to as the message without these attributes, so it is important that our message is personalised to those we wish to engage with. Without this we may be marching too far ahead and be totally disconnected from the audience. Also if the change is something we want to achieve within ourselves we too can get disconnected from our own desire for change — if we cannot contextualise it to our own wellbeing.

We need to connect to our audience/team/ individual for our message to be met with engagement. Engagement starts with people believing you are who you say you are. You must be the change you, or they, want to see.

REMEMBER, CHANGE STARTS WITH YOU, AND OTHERS WILL QUICKLY GET DISCONNECTED IF YOU DO NOT ROLE MODEL THE CHANGE YOU ARE LOOKING TO IMPLEMENT. ALSO REMEMBER YOU CANNOT TALK YOURSELF OUT OF A PROBLEM THAT YOU HAVE BEHAVED YOURSELF INTO. YOU CAN ONLY BEHAVE YOUR WAY OUT WITH THE FORGIVENESS AND ACCEPTANCE OF OTHERS.

MOST OF US WOULD RATHER BE RUINED BY FLATTERY THAN BE BENEFITED BY CRITICISM.

Another aspect of maintaining engagement with an audience or yourself is truthfulness. Truthfulness is a vital ingredient in the maintenance of the link with others and your inner self. Truthfulness is not just a quality of the mind but must reflect all of you; mind, body and soul. If we are lying to ourselves, it is much easier to lie to others. We must openly confront brutal facts about ourselves which may challenge our faith in what we are trying to do.

However, do not be tempted into work arounds. Too often we allow ourselves to be tempted into easy options. People lose faith in us when we lose faith in ourselves. If the truth needs to be 'outed' then so be it. We can never move forward until we challenge the facts about ourselves, forgive ourselves and move on. This way we ensure that people stay with us.

In leadership development programmes that I run, it is critical that leaders work with their teams on a common vision, strategies for the future and that the leader connects to others that they are trying to engage . I often use the acronym **IMPACT** to get my message across. How a leader has impact and maintains engagement is

I In the room. If you are in the room you must be in the room 100%. Too often we are not listening, hearing, responding, engaging with others and it is a very quick way to be seen as rude or not very engaging.

M Model the behaviour you want to see. If you cannot be authentic and immersed in the change you want to see then it is very difficult for people to follow your words rather than your actions.

P Passion and purpose. If you have not got a passion and a purpose, people will find it difficult to understand and contextualise what you are asking. Further, it will be very difficult for you to motivate yourself to be the change you want to see.

A Action orientated. Decisive people help to maintain energy and momentum. People become totally disorientated if they see blockages, meaningless time lags, inappropriate behaviour not being addressed, or the leader being too far ahead or behind their current reality.

C Comedy. I remember being told in my early career, if you are not having fun, you are not doing it right. Do not make fun an agenda item. Make it part of who you are and what you do.

T Trust. Trust. Trust. You must trust yourself and others. If you do not trust, both personally and professionally, then no-one will ever trust you and you can be sure there will always be a chasm between you and others, where people 'Mind the Gap' in case you use it to drop them in.

5 THINGS TO DO SO AS NOT TO GET TOO FAR AHEAD OF OTHERS

1
HAVE A CLEAR AND UNWAVERING GOAL

2
BE THE PERSON NOW YOU WANT TO BE

3
BE TRUTHFUL, TRUSTWORTHY, AND TALENTED

4
COMMUNICATE COMMUNICATE COMMUNICATE UP, SIDEWAYS, DOWN

5
PUT EMOTION AND VULNERABILITY IN ALL CONNECTIONS

WE FIRST MAKE OUR HABITS, AND THEN OUR HABITS MAKE US.

HAVE A PASSIONATE PURPOSE

I recently read the book *I am Malala* by the young girl who was shot by the Taliban. I was so impressed by this child who was so articulate, so bright and so passionate about women's right to an education. I just love passionate people. I love the mix of raw emotion, the light in the eye and the energy and enthusiasm that usually accompanies passion. We often talk about passion and passionate people, but we tend to describe passion without context or meaning. We recognise it in others but many of us do not fully understand the pull of passion. I am just as guilty of this. For many of us passion simply means strong emotions.

PASSION COMES FROM DEEP WITHIN US.

It is not something that can be imposed or mandated from others. Having a passionate purpose compels us to take action and to engage with the world around us.

NOW LET'S NOT MIX PASSION UP WITH HAPPINESS.

Happiness is of the moment. Passion gives us a purpose. Sometimes we have to give up a lot when we pursue our passions and we can be asked to make a significant sacrifice. Passion is about a self-imposed discipline that drives us to persist in the face of enormous obstacles. If passion is integrated into our working lives it can turn stress into stimulus and build energy. Passion, in the sense that I am using it, orients us; it provides us with focus and direction.

5 THINGS TO DO WITH A

PASSIONATE PURPOSE

PURSUE PASSION

Do not be passive. Passionate people explore the world around them and are willing to pursue a goal without fully understanding the path. They pursue and create. They have an unbridled inquisitiveness about anything that impacts on their world. I believe we are all intelligent but that we are sometimes lazy about getting involved and often prefer to be bystanders. Passionate people have an overwhelming urge to engage, to experience for themselves and to test their own capabilities. Passion compels us to act. Are we ready to follow our passion?

CONNECT PASSION

We know that many great ideas come from a Eureka moment. Yet most ideas come from when one idea collides with another idea. Therefore, once we have ignited our passion we must seek out and connect with others who share our passion in a quest for insight that we can bring back into our own domains.

USE YOUR PASSION TO PULL

Passionate people are deeply creative in seeking out and pulling in resources which will help them to pursue their passion. But passion also pulls in another dimension as well. People who pursue their passions inevitably create beacons which attract others who share their passion. Few of these beacons are consciously created; they are by-products of pursuing one's passion. Passionate people share their passions and creations widely. Having a deep passion and purpose will pull people with us.

LET PASSION TAKE YOU THROUGH RISKS

As the saying goes — if we are not making mistakes then we are not stretching ourselves and learning. Passion comes from within and drives us to embrace unexpected opportunities and explore uncharted territories; it does not deal well with prescribed routines and scripts. Passion diminishes our perceptions of risk and amplifies our perceptions of reward. Passion is also about urgency — passionate people have limited patience. If we develop the passion it will drive us forward, regardless of the obstacles put in our way.

HAVE AUTHENTIC PASSION

Truly passionate people have little patience with pretence. They present themselves as they really are because they intuitively understand that is the only way to explore and discover. Passionate people discover and develop a uniquely personal voice that provides a deep sense of meaning and personal identity, shaped by what they contribute to the world and how others build on, and learn from, their contributions. Our passionate identity is not about consumption; it is about shared creation.

BE A

LOOK IN A MIRROR AND ONE THING IS FOR SURE, WHAT WE SEE IS NOT WHO WE ARE.

KEEP ME AWAY FROM THE WISDOM WHICH DOES NOT CRY, THE PHILOSOPHY WHICH DOES NOT LAUGH AND THE GREATNESS WHICH DOES NOT BOW BEFORE CHILDREN.

KAHLIL GIBRAN

This morning my 4 year old son asked me "How do I become a leader?" It suddenly dawned on me that he has inspired me to be a better person, a better father and certainly a better leader. I have gained the humility to recognise that even though I am his father and supposedly the teacher in our relationship, he has been teaching me the entire time. The skills that I have developed and the lessons I have learned with him have been spilling over into my professional life for years.

So, I would like to share vital leadership lessons that I have learned from my son. I have watched him embrace life with an enthusiasm which is infectious and have learned that too often I evaluate before I engage. I have seen him question everything, when I assume that is just the way things are. I have seen him being fearless in his willingness to do new things when often I am fearful. I have loved the way he trusts by default when too often I do it by exception. His loyalty knows no bounds whereas mine is shamefully considered. And when he plays — wow! This is where we can all learn — play is often described as a time when we feel most invigorated and alive. Play isn't just a luxury — it's a necessity. Play is as important to our physical and mental health and well-being as getting sufficient sleep, eating properly and exercise. Play promotes learning, alleviates stress and connects us in an emotional way to others. Play is when learning is easy. Play also teaches us how to manage and transform our 'negative' emotions and experiences. Now, as adults we think play is for children. We after all are powerful, responsible people with big work and important stuff that has no room for irresponsible playfulness. And when we do get leisure time — that time we could allocate to play — we sit in front of TVs, computer screens, drinking wine, refusing to give ourselves permission to play with the joyful abandon of childhood.

I HAVE ALSO SEEN CHILDREN SUCCESSFULLY SURMOUNTING THE EFFECTS OF AN EVIL INHERITANCE. THAT IS DUE TO PURITY BEING AN INHERENT ATTRIBUTE OF THE SOUL.

MAHATMA GANDHI

In my corporate dealings I was always amused by meeting agendas which included the item 'have fun'. I always asked "do I have to wait until that item to have a laugh?" I now run many programmes I call 'edutainment' — education through entertainment — and these are by far our most popular events. People just love to have a laugh, yet work often gets in the way of those real belly laughs!

INNOVATION AND CREATIVITY ARE VITAL INGREDIENTS FOR SUCCESS.

The key driver of innovation and creativity is divergent thinking. Yet we squeeze creativity out of our children through the systems we impose, the rigidity of the educational system and the regulated environments we impose. And that's before they even get to work! Our workplaces reinforce rules, procedures, compliance, playing safe, feudalistic managers and not making mistakes.

Creativity — the idea of original thinking — most often comes when people ask a different question and that's the beauty of the child mind. I refuse to accept that people are not creative. In the workshops I run I am amazed by the unbelievable capability I see when participants are given the licence to be a child again. I think that living in a world in which anything is possible is not the construct of a deranged brain, rather, it is the product of imagination without constraints. Many of us have lost the ability to use our imagination to its full capacity and need to find this capability again.

THINGS TO DO
WHEN BEING A
Child

IT'S OK TO BE CHILDISH!

I cannot plant imagination into leaders. I can, however, provide an environment where their creativity is not just another mess to clean up but something that delivers us to our best selves, the ones that long for risk and illumination and unspeakable beauty. If we sit still long enough, we may hear the call behind boredom. With practice, we may have the imagination to rise up from the emptiness and answer. Adapted and changed from — Nancy H. Blakey.

I see great things in people I coach. However, that greatness is often restrained by walls that are difficult to knock down. Even when we do remove these barriers, we often find that people's thinking remains chained to the past or a set of beliefs which limits them. Be a child, behave like a child, have the wild abandon of a child and the world will be a different place.

BE CONSTANTLY CURIOUS

By nature children are curious, but as we grow we lose that deep dive inquisitiveness. I say that all leaders are intelligent but not all leaders are inquisitive. My son asks lots and lots of questions. That's how he learns. My concern is that when I send him to school he will learn that answers are more important than questions. We must look outside our own domain of expertise, embrace the crazy, the new, the strange and the scary. Only then will we find ideas that challenge our own.

BE AN INDEPENDENT THINKER

Diversity is critical for creativity and innovation, therefore, it is important to seek out points of view different from your own. Yet, do not play follow the leader. There are two new competencies we need: unbridled inquisitiveness and an absorptive capacity. It is no good just being curious, we must synthesise and apply that knowledge. Look to diversity, different domains and crazy people, gather their ideas, challenge them and look for contradictions. If we can solve the contradictions, then we are at our creative best.

KEEP IT SIMPLE

As people go through, and particularly up, organisations they think that they need to prove their intelligence by making things more complex. Simplicity is genius. I beg individuals to make things more simple than complex. It's a myth to think that we have to spontaneously create something that's entirely original and no one ever thought of before. That very rarely, if ever, happens. Almost all ideas come from the collision of ideas. You have an idea, I have an idea. The two ideas collide and now we have a great idea. One of the big principles of creativity is that we don't have to reinvent the wheel, just give it a new spin. So if we can give a new spin to somebody else's idea, then we have done something creative.

CREATE MAGICAL WORLDS

We allow our world to be our world. We allow our thinking, our experiences and our fears to be the walls of the castle in which we live. We accept that what we have is what we have, that the world is round and that our lives are on a straight line journey to an uncertain end. Children do not think like this. They can leap walls, they can change experiences, they have no fears and they are not bound by others. Magic is believing in yourself; if you can do that, you can make anything happen.

CARVE YOUR NAME ON HEARTS, NOT TOMBSTONES. A LEGACY IS ETCHED INTO THE MINDS OF OTHERS AND THE STORIES THEY SHARE ABOUT YOU.

SHANNON L. ALDER

Leaving a
LEGACY

THE MASS OF MEN WORRY
THEMSELVES INTO NAMELESS
GRAVES WHILE HERE AND THERE A
GREAT UNSELFISH SOUL FORGETS
HIMSELF INTO IMMORTALITY.

RALPH WALDO EMERSON

I write this mindset on the day that one of my heroes has died. I have read Nelson Mandela, been in wonder of Mandela and, for a long time, willed Mandela to succeed. As a child of the 60/70s in Ireland I saw, and suffered from, racism in a much more tolerant society than South Africa. This gave me a desire to try to understand more of Mandela's world.

I have read as much as I could on Mandela's life and I love his line "everything is impossible until it is done". I ask leaders many times what is the legacy they want to leave? So what is Mandela's legacy? There was so much to admire about Mandela. I have always been taken by his line "it always seems impossible until it's done" and that relentless focus on the achievement of our goals. I often pose the question to leaders in workshops and coaching: What do you want your legacy to be? Mandela to me was so clear on his values, his principles, with an unshakeable commitment that made people take note of who he was. However, this passion and transparency engaged his audience rather than frightened them, because he demonstrated moral courage, huge courtesy and respect and significant charisma. He gave trust and trusted without question, He spoke as he would want to be spoken to and he treated his friends and his enemies with huge respect, courtesy and of course belief that he could get them to understand what is important in this world: everyone is equal, everyone has rights, everyone should always be embraced by an overwhelming commitment to seeing the best in themselves and in others.

Each of us is given a unique set of gifts and how we choose to use them very much depends on our mindset for life. I am constantly surprised by the different approach some people have towards their home life and their public life.

Many times we mask our feelings and emotions to ensure that no one can pierce our vulnerabilities, and yet that armour is what blocks the virtues of the world from us. In preceding chapters we have talked about our different opportunities to grow and to approach the world with a different attitude. These will bring enormous rewards in our relationships, in our well-being and in our interactions with the world around us.

This last mindset asks us "have we been more than the sum of our individual parts?"

IF YOU WOULD NOT BE FORGOTTEN
AS SOON AS YOU ARE DEAD, EITHER
WRITE THINGS WORTH READING OR
DO THINGS WORTH WRITING.

BENJAMIN FRANKLIN

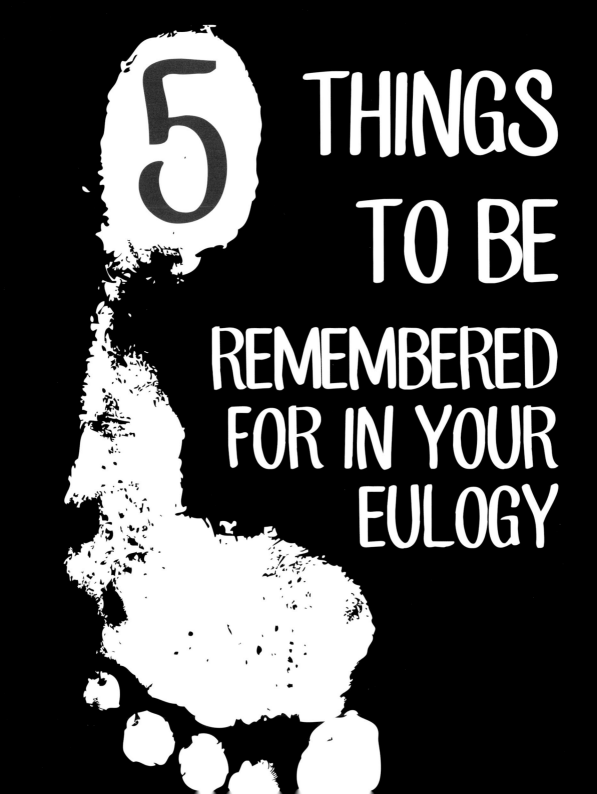

5 THINGS TO BE REMEMBERED FOR IN YOUR EULOGY

A PERSON YOU COULD TRUST

From the work of Stephen M. R. Covey;

1. Demonstrate respect
2. Tell the truth
3. Show loyalty
4. Deliver results
5. Make things right when you're wrong
6. Speak about people as if they were present
7. Clarify expectations
8. Confront reality
9. Hold yourself accountable
10. Listen first
11. Extend trust abundantly
12. Keep commitments

A FRIEND IN TIMES OF NEED

I have discovered that there are many people who want to be associated with you when times are good, but the real friends are those who stick with you through the rough times. A friend of mine captured it best with this proverb.

> *A friend loves at all times, and a brother is born*
> *for a time of adversity.*
> *Proverbs 17:17*

It means that true friends love when there are good and bad times. When you are having problems, a brother (not a literal brother but close friend) is there to help you when you're troubled.

A PERSON WITH VALUES

In my coaching life, I frequently hear executives in their late 40s and early 50s bemoan the fact that they feel trapped, unfulfilled and wishing that they had chosen a different career route. Now these are not under-performers, they regularly hit or achieve their targets, they run great business, they are the beneficiaries of frequent and rapid promotions and are personally rewarded for their efforts. And yet it is at a personal satisfaction level that something is missing and this leaves them with a feeling of under-achievement and a pervasive sense that what they are doing lacks any real meaning.

When it comes to values and leadership, former Medtronic CEO and author of *True North*, Bill George, writes "the values that form the basis for your True North are derived from your beliefs and convictions".

Aligning ourselves toward our True North starts with knowing the values that form the foundation of who we are. No one should tell us what our values should be, that's up to us to decide. What are our values and do we compromise on them?

I AM FUNDAMENTALLY AN OPTIMIST. WHETHER THAT COMES FROM NATURE OR NURTURE, I CANNOT SAY. PART OF BEING OPTIMISTIC IS KEEPING ONE'S HEAD POINTED TOWARD THE SUN, ONE'S FEET MOVING FORWARD. THERE WERE MANY DARK MOMENTS WHEN MY FAITH IN HUMANITY WAS SORELY TESTED, BUT I WOULD NOT AND COULD NOT GIVE MYSELF UP TO DESPAIR. THAT WAY LAYS DEFEAT AND DEATH.

NELSON MANDELA

A PERSON YOU COULD DO BUSINESS WITH

We all want to do business with people we can do business with. A person who is open to engagement, interested in others, seeks new ideas, always looks for a win/win, is trustworthy, authentic, is genuine not just generous, tough but fair, willing to learn and fun to be with. Would people describe us in this way?

A PERSON WHO GAVE ENERGY TO OTHERS

Passionate people, with the right attitude to life, lift those around them. They are a ray of sunshine in any environment. Are you a person who extinguishes a candle or fans a fire? When all is said and done, will people look back and say, "There lived a great person, whose memory will dwell long in this space, for they gave energy, friendship and trust to others, not just in spots, but in a fulfilling way?"

NO LEGACY IS SO RICH AS HONESTY.

WILLIAM SHAKESPEARE

PRIDE AND POWER FALL WHEN THE PERSON FALLS, BUT DISCOVERIES OF TRUTH FORM LEGACIES THAT CAN BE BUILT UPON FOR GENERATIONS.

CRISS JAMI

One of my favourite quotes from Walt Disney is...

IF YOU CAN DREAM IT, YOU CAN DO IT.

The same is true if you wish to change your mindset. I am often asked "How long does it take to change someone's behaviour?" My answer is typically nine months if I am trying to do it for them, or one second if they really want to do it themselves. Basically, we achieve what we believe we can. This does not mean that we do not sometimes slip back to our old ways of behaving. We all have a dark side and it's our attempts to manage these dark sides which define us as a person. If we invest time and effort into changing our mindset, it can lead us to take actions which will change our behaviours. We can look at mindsets in two ways. We can have a fixed mindset where we believe our characteristics are carved in stone. Now this is one extreme, where we just believe we are who we are and that our intelligence, creativity and personality have been defined and cannot be developed. Or we can have a growth mindset, where we believe that we never stop learning and adapting and that we can be whoever we choose to be. Our mindset is the view we adopt of ourselves.

In Carol Dweck's book, *Mindset: The New Psychology of Success*, they show —

We offered four-year-olds a choice: They could redo an easy jigsaw puzzle or they could try a harder one. Even at this tender age, children with the fixed mindset — the ones who believed in fixed traits — stuck with the safe one. "Kids who are born smart don't make mistakes", they told us. And when they looked at the more growth-oriented kids they welcomed the harder puzzle, finding a safer puzzle to be boring.

10
Keys to
UNLOCKING
your full
POTENTIAL

REWRITE YOUR NEGATIVE SCRIPTS - KILL THOSE NEGATIVE THOUGHTS

UNLEARN TO LEARN - RID YOURSELF NOW OF THOSE INHIBITIONS WHICH HOLD US BACK

VIEW YOURSELF THROUGH THE EYES OF OTHERS - DO NOT LET OUR BIASES PREJUDICE US

LISTEN AND LEARN.
BE INQUISITIVE ABOUT OTHERS.
LEARN SOMETHING NEW
EVERY DAY

DON'T JUDGE - REMEMBER IT IS
EASIER TO LABEL THE MISTAKES
OF OTHERS THAN TO RECOGNISE
OUR OWN

GIVE TRUST AND MAKE
CONNECTIONS - REMEMBER
WE CANNOT TALK OURSELVES
OUT OF A PROBLEM WE HAVE
BEHAVED OURSELVES INTO

MAKE MISTAKES - IF WE ARE NOT MAKING MISTAKES WE ARE NOT STRETCHING OURSELVES

CONTINUE DEVELOPING SELF-DISCIPLINE AND SELF-CONTROL - CHANGE ALWAYS STARTS WITH US

DO NOT LIVE IN THE PAST - WE MUST FORGIVE OURSELVES AND MOVE TO WHERE WE WANT TO BE TODAY

10

BE THE PERSON YOU ALWAYS WANTED TO BE - START TODAY BY ADOPTING THE RIGHT MINDSET

The road to change is neither straightforward, nor direct. We will encounter obstacles that challenge our thinking. However, the willingness to learn and hunger for change will deliver the change we want to see. By being the person we want to be, we will become better equipped to discover a new way of living and connecting with others, and to appreciate that we truly are the author of our own lives.

"Go n-éirí an bóthar leat"

ACKNOWLEDGMENTS

Over the years I have written many blogs and white papers, however, *New Mindsets for New Times* is my first venture into book writing. A change for me and it took a whole different mindset. It tested my willingness and ability to take time, change my attitude and be more fearless. Yet I could not have done it without the help of a number of people. I love the vocalisation of ideas and the interaction workshops and conferences bring me and sometimes would say that this is where I learn most. I know people pay to hear what I have to say, but a room full of very bright people always teach me, and challenge my thinking.

I would like to thank all those who attended my workshops and conferences as this is where many of the ideas and thoughts came from.

I would also like to thank the executives I coach and the brilliant coaches who work with us. Too many to name and yet each of you have always given me something different.

I have also worked with some great companies, but want to mention some who have allowed me to try different things. It is in our mistakes that we get the greatest learning and I want to thank some very special individuals who have helped me to learn:

From the opportunity to run a manufacturing site given to me by Chand Mehay; to the great HR team at Nortel Networks where Geoff Merson allowed me to be a proper HR person; to Jonas Prising and Peter Anthony at Manpower who allowed me to run global sales teams.

To Hugo Bagué at Rio Tinto where our coaching model is constantly being challenged and further developed, to Alison Hughes and Cameron Ward who work in the NHS where I am learning more and more each day.

To Peter at Crusoe's in Tynemouth, an oasis of peace on the beach where I often go to write, you probably know more about business than I ever will.

I would also like to thank the draft reading team who probably really wrote this work — Karen Lee, Áine Duffy, Chris Lennie, Andy Laidler, Kate Haven and Jessica Cretu who did rewrites and Jordyn Cartmill who did a magical job on the graphics.

To all of you, my thanks.

To my family; Karen, Eoin, Ciara, Áine & Ethan, my love and thanks from a lucky husband & Dad.

DELETED SCENES

TO BE ADDED TO BOOK TWO

NEW CHAPTER

NEW LIFE

I WILL NOT BE BULLIED BY **MY BRAIN**

BE A WALLFLOWER

BE THE BEST VERSION OF YOU THAT - YOU - CAN BE

HAVE A NORTH AND SOUTH POLE BIAS

FROM ATTITUDE TO ELEVATION

FIRST CAUSES AND ULTIMATE ENDS

MAKE AN OMELETTE WITH BROKEN EGGS

BE LIKE EBENEZER SCROOGE

YOU ARE ALWAYS A WORK IN PROGRESS!

'FORTHRIGHT', 'OUTSPOKEN' AND A 'SMART MAVERICK'.

Conference Review March 2013

Maurice Duffy is founder and CEO of blackswan, a business transformation consultancy that operates globally in over 20 countries. He is respected for his work on leadership, change and transformation, in which he both practices and consults around the world. Maurice personally coaches and mentors a number of Chief Executives and board-level Directors of FTSE 100 and Fortune 500 companies, whilst also sitting as Chair on a number of advisory boards.

Maurice is Irish, married to Karen, lives in the North East of England, has four children – the youngest only four years old – three grandchildren – and two dogs. He is an author and poet, passionate about the positive role change can bring to people's lives, Ireland, Liverpool FC, rugby and family. He is a keen runner, having completed the annual half-marathon Great North Run 14 times, a number of marathons, and is regularly involved in a number of other charitable events and challenges.

BIBLIOGRAPHY

Blakey, N., 'Nurturing Your Child's Creativity', Retrieved January 7, 2014, from http://www.ahaparenting.com

Carroll, L., 'Alice's Adventures in Wonderland and through the Looking Glass' (London: Wordsworth Editions, 2008)

Christakos, G., 'Integrative Problem-Solving in a Time of Decadence' (London: Springer Dordrecht Heidelbeg, 2010)

Coelho, P., 'The Alchemist' (New York: Harper Collins, 1988)

Covey, S. R., 'Everyday Greatness: Inspiration for a Meaningful Life' (USA: Rutledge Hill Press, 2006)

Davenport. T., Beck, J., 'Getting the Attention You Need', Harvard Business Review (September 2000)

Denning, S., 'The Secret Language of Leadership: How leaders Inspire Action Through Narrative' (California: Jossey - Bass, 2007)

Disraeli, B., 'Coningsby or the New Generation' (London: Longman Green & Co, 1844)

Dweck, C. S., 'Mindset: The New Psychology of Success' (New York: Random House, 2006)

Flores, L. G., 'Executive Career Advancement: How to Understand the Politics of Promotion' (Indiana: AuthorHouse, 2009)

George, B., Sims, P., 'True North; Discover Your Authentic Leadership' (California: Jossey–Bass, 2007)

Gibran, K., 'The Wisdom of Gibran' (London: Bantam Books, 1973)

Grad, M., 'Charisma: How to get "That Special Magic"' (UK: Wilshire Book Company, 1986)

Hacala, S., 'Saving Civility: 52 Ways to Tame Rude, Crude and Attitude for a Polite Planet' (USA: Skylight Paths Publishing, 2011)

Heo, S. E., 'Reconciling Enemy States in Europe and Asia' (Hampshire: Palgrave Macmillan, 2012)

Holmes, R. L., 'The Ethics of Nonviolence' (London: Bloomsbury Acedemic, 2013)

Jami, C., 'Venus in Arms' (CreateSpace Independent Publishing Platform, 2012)

Karkanis, P. G., 'Thoughts for Meaningful Life' (Indiana: AuthorHouse, 2008)

Kipling, R., 'A Choice of Kipling's Verse' (London: Faber & Faber, 1963)

Kumar, P. P., 'Inclusive Growth' (2nd Edition) (Pratheek, 2011)

Mandela, N., 'Long Walk to Freedom' (London: Little, Brown Book Group, 2008)

McCauley Bush, P., 'Transforming Your STEM Career Through Leadership and Innovation' (USA: Academic Press, 2012)

Naisbitt, J., 'Mind Set! Eleven Ways to Change the Way You See—and Create—the Future' (New York: Harper Collins, 2006)

Parthasarathy, A., 'Vedanta Treatise The Eternities' (A. Parthasarathy, 1979)

Pattakos, A., 'Prisoners of our Thoughts: Viktor Frankl's Principles at Work' (California: Berrett-Koehler, 2004)

Pradeep, A. K., 'The Buying Brain: Secrets for Selling to the Subconscious Mind' (USA: John Wiley & Sons, 2010)

Ramji, M. T., 'The Concept of Personality in the Educational thought of Mahatma Gandhi' (National Council of Educational Research and Training, 1969)

Rao, M. S., 'Soft Skills: Enhancing Employability' (New Delhi: IK International Publishing House, 2010)

Rohe, D., Larson, J. A., 'On Leaving a Legacy' in Larson, J. A., (ed.) 'Management Engineering: A Guide to Best Practices for Industrial Engineering in Health Care' (USA: Productivity Press, 2013)

Shakespeare, W., 'The Dramatic Works of William Shakespeare - Volume 1' (George Bell and Son, 1892)

Shaw, G. B., 'Man and Superman: A Comedy and a Philosophy' (USA: Wildside Press, 2008)

Stephens, R., 'On Top of the World' (London: Macmillan, 1994)

Taleb, N., 'The Black Swan: The Impact of the Highly Improbable' (London: Penguin, 2008)

Vickers, A., Bavister, S., Smith, J., 'Personal Impact: Make a Powerful Impression Wherever You Go: What it Takes to Make a Difference' (UK: Pearson Life, 2008)

Wiseman, R., 'The Luck Factor: The Scientific Study of the Lucky Mind' (London: Arrow Books, 2004)

Yousafzai, M., 'I am Malala: The Girl Who Stood Up for Education and Was Shot by the Taliban' (Weidenfeld & Nicolson, 2013)

Designed by Jordyn Cartmill

Edited by Kate Haven and Jessica Cretu